THE WEL

Preface

The late Mr Howgrave-Graham was approached by the present editor several years ago about the possibility of his writing a book on the Wells Clock for publication by the Friends of Wells Cathedral for the use of visitors and for the information of local residents, too. This he readily agreed to do, but for various reasons and Mr Howgrave-Graham's multifarious other occupations and interests nothing further came of the project.

His widow has readily given permission for extracts to be taken from his book *Peter Lightfoot, Monk of Glastonbury, and the Old Clock at Wells,* Glastonbury, 1922, and from the text of a lecture given before a joint meeting of the Newcomen Society and Antiquarian Horological Society in 1954, since printed in the *Transactions of the Newcomen Society,* Vol. xxix, pp.137-149. The Secretary of the Newcomen Society has very kindly given permission to quote quite extensively from that paper. Both Mr Howgrave-Graham and the editor would wish also to thank Mr John Harvey for his generous help.

The photographs of the works of the clock are Crown copyright and have been kindly supplied by the Director of the Science Museum, London. The photograph of the outside quarter-jacks was taken at the beginning of this century by Phillips' City Studio, Wells. All other photographs of the clock were taken specially for this booklet by Jonathan Robertson. The photograph of the Christus is by S. W. Kenyon of Wellington.

In the following pages paragraphs or sentences which have been re-worded or substantially re-written by the editor, and additions of his own, are enclosed within square brackets, leaving the bulk of the booklet in Mr Howgrave-Graham's own words.

L.S.C.

Description of the Clock as seen inside the Church

[The clock-face and two of the automata can be seen in the North transept of the Cathedral. The works were undoubtedly made in about 1390 (see page 7 below), and the face and some of the equipment belong to the same time. Here follows a general description of what the visitor sees.

The outside circle, 6 feet 4 inches in diameter, shows the hours—two sets of 12 hours—on the right side going down from 1 to 12 midnight at the bottom, and up on the left side to 12 noon at the top. The 12 is in each case represented by a floriated cross in red. The space between the numerals is adorned with stars painted on a blue background, representing the night sky.

What appears to be a large star is in fact the sun going round the earth (which is in the centre of the dial), and this acts as the hour hand. It does, in fact, exactly correspond to the apparent position of the actual sun outside—at the top of the sky at midday, sinking towards the West in the evening, and in the antipodes at midnight.

The second circle shows ordinary minutes, 1 to 60, in arabic numerals. The small star serves as the minute hand. So it is just as easy to tell the time by this clock as on a modern clock or wrist-watch.

The third circle has arabic numerals up to 30. A trident- or buckle-shaped pointer attached to the innermost disc, which we here call the "moon-plate", points to the figure which represents the date of the lunar month, i.e. the number of days since the New Moon. The "Trident" possibly represents a crescent moon with pointer in the middle.

The circular hole beside this pointer reveals a golden moon] beginning with a gold crescent, which grows until the whole opening is backed by gold at full moon, and in due course wanes.

[But this is not all. In addition to waxing and waning it is also continually turning, so that it represents the exact appearance of the moon at any time. The manner in which this is contrived is ingenious. The ring marked with the number of lunar days] revolves once in 24 hours, and the moonplate is carried round with it at a slightly slower speed; the small difference is sufficient to make it lag 12° in 360°, the result being that the "buckle-shaped" pointer attached to it moves backwards with reference to the lunar days, and indicates in a counter-clockwise direction an advance of one day out of the 30 lunar days during every 24 hours. The arrangement is ingeniously contrived so that the ring of the lunar days revolves once in a day, while the disc is carried round in the opposite direction once in a month.

As, however, the time of real rotation of the Moon about the Earth is not exactly 30 days, this clock, like others having lunation, needs to be adjusted once in a month.

Phoebe

Opposite to the moon-opening on the innermost dial is a small circular medallion, on which is painted a quaint female figure symbolic of the Moon (Phoebe), a scroll partly surrounding the figure bears the inscription *Sic peragrat Phoebe* in bold characters such as were prevalent in Italy during the Renaissance, when they gradually spread through Europe and provided the prototype for modern printing founts. This inscription may be rendered "So progresses Phoebe". The medallion is pivoted and provided with a counterweight so that during the daily rotation of the moon-plate the figure of Phoebe always remains upright. I think this little figure has no parallel elsewhere.

The Earth

Finally we have at the centre of the dial a ball surrounded by a wavy petal-like carving of the kind which symbolised clouds and the sky. This central piece represents the four elements earth, air, fire and water.

Inscription

[One more inscription remains to be noted and that gives the key to the whole clock-face. Around the moon-plate are the words *Sphericus archetypum globus hic monstrat microcosmum* which may be translated, "This circular dial represents the actual universe in miniature." That accounts for the sun and the stars, and the moon, and the earth at the centre (as it was then visualised). It also explains the figures of angels in the four corners of the square outside the main circle, each holding a man's head puffing, to represent the four cardinal winds.] To summarise the astronomical side of the horologe, we have the Earth at the centre surrounded by the spheres of air (and fire?), the Moon revolving round it in strict accordance with the Ptolemaic conceptions of her diurnal and proper motions, the sun making his journey round the earth once in 24 hours, the starry firmament outside these and the four cardinal winds in their traditional places at the corners.

The Wells clock, then, is not a mere clock: it is essentially a model illustrating fundamental mediaeval conceptions of creation and the universe.

When the Clock Strikes

In the triforium above the clock-face and northward of it is a large oaken figure that strikes bells at the hours and quarters with its heels. [This figure also strikes the hour on the bell hanging in front of him, using the hammer held in his right hand. He also holds a hammer in his left hand, and the left elbow is jointed, but this does not move. With each stroke of the hour-bell he slightly turns his head as if listening carefully to the harmonics.] This quaint and grave figure is locally known as Jack Blandifer [or Blandiver. He] appears superficially to be of Charles I period because of the face-painting; but his hair and garments suggest late 14th century to me.

[Jack Blandifer and his sentry-box were formerly in the first opening of the triforium on the North wall, and are so shown by Britton c.1823. His present position makes him easier to see for one watching the other automata of the clock, and also simplifies the transmission of wires operating him.]

The Horsemen

Above the pediment of the interior face is a wooden turret in the Gothic style, standing in the midst of an octagonal battlemented platform arranged to serve the purpose of lists for the famous little horsemen who tourney round the turret every hour, driven by a mechanism with a separate weight. [The mechanism operating the jousting knights now works at every quarter-hour, aided by an electric motor installed in 1968. This was partly because the transept became overcrowded by spectators on the hour; also because the disappointment was so great of those who arrived a few minutes late and missed it. So now, as Jack Blandifer kicks his quarters the knights bestir themselves, and] rush round in contrary directions, and charge each other with so much ferocity that one unfortunate is felled at each encounter, and has barely time to recover his upright position before he is again knocked down with resounding clatter upon his horse's back. The other three fight four times an hour unscathed.

[The horsemen appear to be wearing a variety of costumes. One] has a hood with ears to it, one is nondescript, and another wears the civil costume of James I or Charles I, with falling collar, striped doublet, peaked beard and moustache. [One undoubtedly] has a helmet, though the date is difficult to fix. In his hand is a spear. The figure approaching him from the left carries a broken spear or short sword and is mounted on a spindle, so that when the helmeted adversary smites him he falls backwards flat on his horse. On passing behind the turret he is automatically set up again, only to receive another "knock-out blow", and so on, in rapid succession during several encounters, with most comic effect. He is the hero with the "eared hood", and it is difficult to see what other head-gear can be intended, unless it is a grotesque helmet, though well-known antiquaries tell me that they never encountered a head-dress of this type.

The effect of all the figures is most quaint, and the ears on the hood, if such it be, give the long-suffering wearer some resemblance to a dormouse. The turret, the platform, and the small arched and painted wooden screen which partly fill the space between them and the stonework, and through which the horsemen pass back and forth in their career, are all of early perpendicular type, quite compatible with the date [c.1390], and show that both they and the mechanism for carrying round the figures are contemporary with the clock, even if one or more figures have been renewed. There are, I think, two distinct periods for the horsemen, and the two who actually come to blows seem to me to be early, though there is nothing definite for dating them. I am inclined to think that the other two, who only ride, are later.

The Date

[The Communars' account rolls at Wells survive for the years 1327/8, 1343/4 and 1392/3 in addition to later ones. The roll for 1392/3 has the critical entry: *In stipendiū custodientis la Clokk ꝑ annū Xs* (Clock-keeper's wages for the year, 10 shillings). There was no reference to any clock or its keeper in the account rolls for 1327/8 or 1343/4, but the clock-keeper features in all the 36 extant Communars' rolls from 1392 to 1560. It is clear, therefore, that the clock was made sometime between 1344 and 1392.

The Communars' accounts relate mainly to wages. Repairs to the clock would appear in the Fabric accounts. Of the earliest extant Fabric roll, for the year 1391/2, only half survives: the part giving expenses having been torn off and lost. Subsequent extant Fabric rolls mention repairs to the chime in 1480/1; for changing the clock bell and making a "wyndelas" for "le Chyme" in 1492/3; for mending a wheel and "trockee de le Chyme" in 1500/01; for general repairs to the clock (3/4d); mending the chymes, 10d; mending the chymes 3d; making a hammer for the chimes (*unius lez ham' ꝑ lez chymes*) 5s—all in 1549/50.

The account rolls after 1560 make regular mention of the clock, but excerpts are not necessary here, because there is sufficient evidence above to show that the clock of which we have the first mention in 1392 remained in use continuously from then on.

The Lightfoot Legend

In the 18th century a story was started which has been repeated with incredible persistence ever since to the effect that this clock was built by Peter Lightfoot, a monk, for Glastonbury Abbey, and was stolen and brought to Wells when the Abbey was dissolved in 1539. The earliest occurrence of this story that I have been able to trace is in Collinson's *History and Antiquities of Somerset,* published in 1791. Since then the legend has grown so as to make Lightfoot the maker of the existing clocks at Exeter Cathedral and Wimborne Minster as well as of that at Wells.

Our knowledge of Peter Lightfoot is confined to one mention by John Leland writing in 1540, who says of the clock which he saw at Glastonbury: "Peter Lightfote the monk made this clock", and a statement by John of Glaston in his history of the abbey, who says that a clock was fitted up there in the time of Adam of Sodbury who was Abbot from 1323 to 1334.

It is obvious that this cannot be the Wells clock which was in position in Wells by 1392 and cannot be the one seen by Leland at Glastonbury in 1540. Canon C. M. Church writing in 1909* made this quite clear, yet the foolish legend has persisted. For reasons given below it is extremely unlikely that the Wells clock was made by Peter Lightfoot at all, who seems to have flourished 60 years earlier. The other clocks ascribed to Lightfoot are referred to below (pages 19, 20).

The Salisbury Clock

In Salisbury Cathedral is a clock once again in working order thanks to the efforts of Mr T. R. Robinson of Bristol. This clock is now generally regarded as the oldest working mechanical clock. The Salisbury accounts for 1386 provided for] the building of a house to accommodate the keeper of the clock. [The works of the Salisbury clock are almost identical with those of the Wells clock, with only a few later improvements on the latter.] The aesthetic identity of treatment at Salisbury and Wells is such that photographs of corresponding parts have to be labelled for distinction when put side by side.

We were confronted, then, with two clocks from the same maker, each with a late 14th century date but with no certainty as to earlier existence. The next step was to seek for some connection between Salisbury and Wells. Having decided to investigate the histories of all likely officials I began with the bishop and, to my surprise, he seemed to provide a probable key to the matter at once. Bishop Erghum, a foreigner who was consecrated at Bruges, was at Salisbury from 1375-88, having been Chancellor of the Duchy of Lancaster for John of Gaunt.

Mr John Harvey has sent me the following information which I abbreviate: Erghum was a prominent supporter of Richard II's government and was evidently much at court where he would have the best chance of meeting the latest craftsmen and ideas. The important fact is that he was translated to Bath and Wells in 1388 and remained its bishop until 1400. Is it not highly probable that he employed craftsmen for Salisbury and employed them again for Wells, possibly taking them with him? And is it not at least possible that they were the three "orologiers" Johannes and Willelmus Vrieman and Johannes Lietuyt of Delft invited to England in 1368 by Edward III? [The reference here is to

---

* *S.A.S. (Proceedings of Somerset Archaeological Society),* 1v, 1909, ii, 97-103.

After the "knock-out" blow

NEQUID PEREAT

the *Calendar of Patent Rolls,* Edward III, Vol. xiv, 105, where protection and safe-conduct for a year are granted to these three orlogiers on coming into the realm to practise their art. While the safe-conduct was only for one year, instances exist of aliens engaged in other trades being so licensed and staying for life.

But in view of our present knowledge of clocks built in England from 1280 onwards, it is likely that the maker of the Salisbury and Wells clocks was English.*

Dating of the Parts

Having established that the Salisbury clock was made in 1386 and the Wells clock soon after by the same craftsmen, it would be well to consider which parts appear to belong to the original clock and what has apparently been added later. The mechanism is discussed further on (pages 17-18). Let us take the various parts in the order in which they have been described.

The Clock-face. The colours and details of the dials are exactly as shown by John Carter in 1794† and in Edward John Carlos' MS book of 1824 in the Cathedral Library. We know they were repainted in 1727§ but no one has noted any record of subsequent repainting. The black-letter Roman numerals of the hour dial,] painted on large circular tablets are of fine and bold Gothic character, but provide no definite evidence of date. They belong to pre-reformation times and are probably part of the original work. If they are renewals they almost certainly follow the original design.

The Arabic numerals of the day and minute rings appear to belong to the 17th century, having presumably been repainted, and it may be that the words *Sic peragrat Phoebe* were renewed at the same time. [However, this] inscription appears to be of the 16th century, and it is possible that the whole medallion is late, but far more probable that the lettering has been repainted over old work.

[The] legend in Gothic letters [*Sphericus archetypum globus hic monstrat microcosmum*] surrounding the moon-disc is probably an untouched feature of the original clock, the lettering being of a style near to the date 1400. Strangely enough, Dr Armitage Robinson, [sometime] Dean of Wells (but of Westminster at the time), discovered a reference by John Flete, a monk of Westminster Abbey, 1420-1425, to a similar inscription on the Abbey pavement. The words quoted from the monk John Flete refer to certain decorations on a pavement laid down in front

---

* see C. F. C. Beeson, *English Church Clocks 1280-1850,* Phillimore, 1971.

† BL Add MS 29932 f 112.

§ Fabric accounts, 1727/8. (*Cal. MSS.* ii, 519).

of the High Altar at Westminster in the time of Abbot Ware A.D. 1268, and are as follows: *Sphericus archetypum globus hic monstrat macrocosmum.*

This inscription surrounded a representation of the Ptolemaic Universe and the translation of it makes plain good sense: "This rounded globe represents the Macrocosm (great Universe) its archetype."

Jack Blandifer. At a cursory glance he would certainly be assigned to the reign of Charles I, but a careful examination shows details of costume that might be earlier, and his late appearance may be due chiefly to his face having been repainted in the first half of the 17th century. His hat has some resemblance to types of the late 14th and early 15th centuries, and the full sleeves narrowing at the wrist look mediaeval. A puzzling feature is his hair, the conventional treatment of which has a mediaeval appearance, though the fashion suggests a later date. His shoes are of late cut, but his hinged legs may well have been renewed, making them valueless as a guide. The arched wooden sentry-box in which he sits is of the depressed four-centred style, and may be late Mediaeval, Tudor or even Stuart. The fact that the original works have exactly the right provision for the full performance of this jack certainly suggests that if he personally does not belong to the original clock a predecessor carried out the same duties. [It seems reasonable to hold] the view that he belongs to the 15th or late 14th century and has been repainted and repaired.

The Platform, Turret and Stone Screen

The wooden platform round which the four warriors charge has beautiful foliage on the underside, which I assigned to the latter half of the 14th century. This treatment of leaves did not prevail for a very long period. The little tower, through which the warriors charge, has battlement-ornaments.

The clock dial is so adapted to the stone screen that they are almost certainly parts of one scheme. The master-mason, William of Wynford, was paid for three days at Wells in 1391 and one of his subordinates, Thomas Maidstone, was there in 1388-9 for work on the south-west tower. This would not preclude minor works being carried out, and Mr Colchester and Mr Harvey, who have related these records to the building, are almost certain that the screen is of Wynford's design. It has battlement-cresting [identical with that of the south-west tower already mentioned.*

The works were] protected behind mediaeval painted boarding ornamented with what appear to be red and white roses and foliage [visible in the Virgers' office. This] painting may belong to a later period, [possibly to the time when the outside clock face was added.

---

* The stylistic evidence for the dating of the Wells clock is given in a letter from Mr John Harvey in the *Horological Journal,* vol. c, no, 1201 (October 1958), pp. 654 and 658.

The Outside Clock

Nothing has been said so far of the outside clock, sometimes referred to as "the modern clock", since it seems to be a century later than the inside dial and the works that operate it. Here] outside the north transept are two other quarter-jacks, four feet in height, of solid oak and finely carved. They strike the bells with axes, each figure being turned bodily for the purpose through a small angle about a vertical spindle. [These figures were carefully examined by Lt. Col. J. R. Bramble, FSA, in 1909.* His description has been very kindly revised by Mr Claude Blair, FSA, of the Victoria and Albert Museum, in the light of modern knowledge, but without his being able to examine the figures themselves at close quarters:—

> "Each wears a complete suit of 'Gothic' plate armour. The breastplate is formed of an upper and a lower part, of which the latter overlaps the former, curving up to a blunt point at the top of the chest where it is secured by a strap and buckle. Attached to the lower edge is a skirt (*tonlet*) formed of overlapping horizontal hoops, rather like a Venetian blind. Suspended from the lowest lame by two straps and buckles each are two elegantly-fluted pointed plates (*tassets*), protecting the fronts of the thighs. Two similar, but smaller, plates (*hindtassets*) are at the rear. Between the tassets at the front can be seen part of the dagged lower edge of the mail skirt (*fauld*) worn under the tonlet. On No. 1 [the figure on the spectator's left] there is an orifice on the right of the breastplate which may have been where the lance-rest was attached.
>
> The arms are protected by tubular *vambraces* with shell-shaped *cowters* at the elbows (these are visible only on the inner arms, the others being obliterated by the blocks of elm long since attached to them). The shoulders are covered by *pauldrons* of moderate size, fluted in a similar manner to the tassets. No. 1 has four flutings and the pauldron on his right shoulder is very unusual in being larger than the other. The normal arrangement was for the left side to be more heavily reinforced because the lance was couched across the horse's neck, so that contestants came together left side to left side.
>
> The legs are protected by *cuisses* (on the thighs) and *greaves* (on the lower legs), joined over the knees by articulated *poleyns* each secured at the rear by a large strap and buckle. The feet are covered by articulated pointed *sabatons.*
>
> On each figure's head is a helmet of the kind known as a *salet,* with its moveable visor raised, accompanied by a separate chin-piece (*bevor*). The edges are bordered by dome-headed rivets which served to secure the lining on the inside. The visor of No. 1 is elegantly fluted and that of No. 2 plain. The crests, probably of wood, are gone, but their supports remain.

---

* *S.A.S.,* lv, 1909, ii, 101-3.

The gauntlets are made of overlapping plates covering only the backs of the hands. On No. 1 the cuff is pointed; on No. 2 the upper plate is slightly curved.

On No. 1 the photograph appears to have brought out the diagonal line of the sword-belt, probably painted and not carved.

The effigies are four feet in height from heel to the top of the salet. They are decidedly graceful with expressive features and marked individuality.

The style of the armour on the figures can be compared with that found on a number of alabaster effigies which are normally dated to the 1470's, for example at Melbury Sampford and Puddletown, Dorset."

It may perhaps be considered a pity that they always stand with their "backs to the audience", so that their faces are not seen.]

The exterior dial, like the interior one, was originally divided into [two series of 12 hours] but it has been replaced by a comparatively modern twelve-hour face bearing the emblems of the Evangelists. [The old face, with a single hour-hand—also terminating in a representation of the sun, similar to that inside—is shown in E. J. Carlos's MS of 1824 in the Cathedral Library. The numerals were fine Roman capitals. The four Evangelists were there then as now, and are also shown in John Carter's drawing of 1794.

Above the clock painted on the stonework is the motto *NE QVID PEREAT,* meaning "Let nothing be lost", and was aptly adopted as the motto of the Somerset Record Society. Here it refers probably both to time ("Don't waste a minute") and to the fabric ("Don't let it fall into decay"). It is a reminder, too, of that sentence which Dean Malden said in his farewell sermon he had always used as his guiding principle: "Keep that which is committed to thy trust" (1 Tim. 6.20). as referring both to the Cathedral and to the Christian faith.

Mechanism

The clock at Wells is at present operated by a movement dating only from 1880, made by Gillett and Bland, Steam Clock Factory, Croydon. This movement is the second replacement. The original works were removed to the Undercroft and replaced by a modern substitute in 1838. This, however, proved unsatisfactory and had to be replaced after just over 40 years. In 1871 the original works were removed to the old Patent Office Museum in London and put into going order by the straightening of the old wheels and the fitting of a few new brass wheels. These works were transferred from the Patent Office Museum to the Science Museum at South Kensington in about 1883. They are included in the Science Museum pamphlet *50 Things To See.* If, as has been suggested from time to time, the works were returned to Wells and

replaced in their original position in the triforium so as to operate the clock once more, it would be impossible for the public to view them, whereas in the Science Museum they are accessible to all. It has even been suggested that the works should be set in motion in the transept of the Cathedral. But as from this position they could not operate the clock face or the automata, there would be no gain; and it would be simply a case of turning the Cathedral into a museum.

The mechanism measures 31 x 44½ x 47¼ inches] and is entirely made of forged iron fastened by mortice and tenon and cotter, without any screws. The wrought-iron wheels in the time-keeping part of the mechanism are about half-an-inch thick, and one, having ninety teeth, is as much as two feet in diameter; the pinions are of "lantern" form and all working parts are a wonder of accuracy and truth.

A great wheel in the striking train has 64 teeth, is three-quarters of an inch thick and more than 32 inches in diameter.

The striking movement is driven by two separate weights, each acting on its own drum, one being for the two quarter-strokes and the other for the hours; thus it will be seen that there are three weights requiring to be wound up. The striking gear works on the locking-plate principle still largely employed in French striking clocks.

Originally the clock was controlled by a verge-and-balance escapement; but at some time subsequent to the application of the pendulum to clocks by Galileo in the middle of the seventeenth century a pendulum and anchor were fitted in place of the balance and verge.

The verge is a vertical rod, having two pallets which engage alternately with the teeth of the crown wheel. It is suspended by a cord to decrease the wear on the bottom pivot and at its upper end it carries the balance, provided with weights placed equi-distantly on either side of the verge and hung from notches cut in the bar so that the distance from the centre can thus be altered and the moment of inertia of the balance made adjustable for regulation. Rotation of the wheel-work can only take place by producing a slow vibratory motion of the balance by means of the pallets.

[Some of the late alterations to the works are due to Thomas Bilbie of Chew Stoke, described as "Clockmaker and Belfounder", who in accordance with the agreement signed on 22 July 1742 "shall and will repair amend and put in good order the said Clock and Chimes and shall and will find all and every the materials necessary to compleat and finish the said Work and shall and will make all new Chime Hammers and squares and place and put new Teeth and Pinnions in the Room and place of the Stars and Shall and will new turn the Wheels and make new Levit Holes and also make the wheels with Lantern heads of Brass . . . He the said Thomas Bilbie shall and will place and put up the said Clock and Chimes in such manner and Form so as the said Clock shall go twenty six Hours at one time and one winding up." For this he was paid £26 5s on August 1st 1742 and £5 on the August 1st following.*]

* Ledger 1740-1760, page 92. (*Cal. MSS.* ii, 539)

A Comparison with the Salisbury Clock

The Salisbury frame is simple and rectangular with corner standards of buttress type set at 45° and with four substandards and top and bottom medial cross-bars. If we put a quarter-striking mechanism into the hour-striking compartment of Salisbury we should have a near copy of the main part of the Wells movement, and if we now added an extraneous hour-striking movement on the left and at the front this would give us the Wells clock complete as it was before there were trifling minor additions. The whole front is 5ft. 3in., the main frame is about 3ft. 9in., square and the extension is about 1ft. 9in. square. The height is 4ft.

The going train at Salisbury is wound by an elegant three-spoke wheel with a rim of circular section to be gripped, no doubt, as one grips the steering wheel of a car. It might be a renewal; Wells has a later addition for this purpose. The strike movement was wound by a later leaf pinion, the only one and doubtless replacing spokes.

The locking plate is external at Salisbury and internal at Wells; an improvement in orderliness. I have dealt fully [elsewhere] with the Salisbury striking movement, showing its primitive character, the resulting uncertainty of exactitude in striking, and the ingenious remedial arrangements added to gain precision. At Wells we have the highly developed double-lever, which gives precision without added devices.

Did the makers invent quarter-striking between their Salisbury and Wells jobs, or did they learn this from foreigners who knew how it worked at Rouen or elsewhere on the Continent? Or did they know it all along but omit it at Salisbury because Erghum had less to spend or had not developed the enthusiasm which led to the sumptuous dial and automata at Wells?

One small detail suggests a possible refinement in Wells as compared with Salisbury: The space cut out to give freedom for the passage of the verge is square at Salisbury and nicely rounded concentrically at Wells.

[The Wells movement operated (as does also its modern replacement)

1 the inside dials;
2 the inside quarter-jack (Jack Blandifer);
3 the horsemen;
4 the hour-bell at the top of the central tower;
5 the outside dial;
6 the outside quarter-jacks (knights).

While at a quick glance the old works appear simple, their intricacy is proved by the failure of the replacement movement of 1838, and by the complicated nature of the modern works of 1880. Mechanical engineers have asked themselves why the ingenuity and skill used to devise and construct a clock of this kind were never put to practical uses at that time, such as for spinning and weaving wool. One may speculate on the possible sequence of events if the industrial revolution in Britain had come in Richard II's reign instead of 400 years after.

Who Saw the Clock?

It is doubtful if the public had access to the transept when the clock was installed: certainly they were not admitted to this part fifty years earlier. Moreover, judging from the donations in the various offertory boxes about the Cathedral, the number of pilgrims and visitors was small.

Probably the sole purpose of the interior clock was to ensure that canons, vicars and choristers started services punctually. Only the hour-bell in the high tower was for the benefit of the populace.]

Other Old Clocks

Wimborne Minster. There is a simple astronomical dial in which a spherical moon rotates round a central earth in the synodic period, and one half is painted so that it waxes and wanes correctly. The machinery for this is in a wooden case decorated in a style which I have shown to be 17th century, and would call Jacobean. Three angel-heads appear to support it; but are not of a Gothic type. Two trumpeting angels of renaissance character stand on the case, and between them has been placed a meaningless and ugly ornament. More ridiculous is the attribution of the movement to Lightfoot. Its late date is easily seen in its obvious construction for pendulum control, its arrangement of three units in a row in a continuous frame, its use of vertical strap-standards expanding outwards at the bottom to greater width as they do at Winchester Cathedral, St Cross and elsewhere in late work, its assembly by square screw-nuts, its neat and sophisticated wheel-work and its clumsy finials like four-petalled lilies, which are screwed on to the corner standards.

Sherborne Abbey. In the same county is a clock complete with lilies and obviously from the same workshop; the two are almost identical. We have to thank Mr Robinson for his discovery that both are from the end of the 18th century, and by a certain William Monk, not to be confused with that 14th-century monk of Glastonbury.

Exeter Cathedral. The case of Exeter is greatly complicated by the long series of account rolls showing alterations and repairs, and here, as elsewhere, evidence of the existence of an early clock has been assumed as proof of the great age of what remains. The going and striking parts are framed by weak and degenerate members resting on feeble little feet and the spiralled finials, so characteristic of late work and so easily wrought, are almost standard practice in the 17th century clocks I have seen in Strasbourg and Germany where in the 16th century they are sometimes made more dignified by changing width which spreads them out into spiralled scrolls.

The quarter-part, oddly perched on the top of the larger frame, puzzles me. It is solid and altogether a little heavy, with poor mouldings which I should judge to be 17th century, but I should hesitate to dogmatise more than to exclude it from the 14th century group and to doubt a pre-reformation origin.

Harvey sums up the records as set forth in my paper in *Archaeologia** to the following effect: A horologe existing in 1284 was superseded by a clock of new pattern in 1376; this gave constant trouble and in 1423 an entirely new clock was made. He is inclined to think that the present astronomical dial belongs to the 1423 clock and the remains of the cresting are quite in keeping with this.

Ottery St Mary. The astronomical dial is of the Exeter and Wimborne type. It had for the 24-hour ring a small floriated sub-pointer for which Mr J. J. Hall substituted a sphere or disc. It was painted with stars and the corner areas in the square case were diapered. All this Mr Hall painted out though he afterwards expressed regrets. The loft, which appears to me late, he boldly called the clock-loft of Bishop Grandisson, 1327-69, and for the movement he proclaimed the date 1327 or very soon after. There is no foundation for any of these attributions, and most certainly the clock is not of that period. In the clock-loft is an interesting and venerable movement with the usual late characteristics of screw-fastening and rather thin and weak members. The bent-over finials are exceptionally feeble and there is nothing of the grand style to mark it as earlier than the 16th or 17th century.

[The **Cassiobury Park** clock (British Museum), **Dover Castle** (Science Museum) and **Quickswood** clocks may belong to the 14th or early 15th century, but might be a century later.]

---

* *Archaeologia,* vol. lxxvii for 1927 (1928), 257-312, which has some good photographs of details of the Wells clock.

The striking mechanism

Rouen. It seems that the great city clock at Rouen is the oldest known remaining example retaining, in great part, its original wheels though converted to pendulum control. It was the work of Jean de Felains in 1379 and was going until 1929 when the municipality electrified everything and allowed this magnificent movement to stop after 550 years.

Dijon. The Dijon movement was brought from Courtrai after the battle of Roesbeke in 1382. The town was pillaged and the Duke of Burgundy saved the famous clock and the inscribed hour-bell to offer to the town of Dijon which had furnished a thousand men at arms for the campaign.

The splendid iron structure at Dijon may have been at work at any unrecorded time before its reception at Dijon and we must therefore leave the question of priority as between this and the Rouen clock unsettled; in any case later renewals have left little but the frame as original.

Strasbourg.* The clock now at work in the cathedral is housed in an elaborate and soaring architectural structure much of which including paintings, belongs to the astronomical clock designed and calculated by the mathematician, Conrad Dasypodius (1574) and constructed by the famous clockmaker Isaac Harbrecht. It was partially destroyed in 1789.

In 1842 Jean Baptiste Schilgue undertook the reconstruction and elaboration of the marvellous clock now giving the time in two reckonings, the times of sunrise and sunset; the dates of all the moveable ecclesiastical events of the year; the golden number; the dominical letter and other data.

The Christus

[Beneath the dial in Wells Cathedral a wooden carving of Christ the Redeemer was placed in 1956 as a reminder that this is not a museum or a toy-shop. The figure, especially designed for this position, was carved out of yew by E. J. Clack, who carved also the Wells crib figures and the "Expulsion from Eden" in the Palace grounds. It was exhibited at the Royal Academy in 1955, and was given, as recorded on a stone beneath, in memory of the long service in the diocese of Prebendary T. L. Sissmore.]

---

* This short extract about the Strasbourg clock is taken by permission from Mr Howgrave-Graham's much fuller account of the Strasbourg clocks in his *The Cathedrals of France,* Batsford, 1959, 187-8.